CONNECT
LIKE A
B■SS

Developing The Soft Skills
You Need To Take Your Career
To The Next Level

RAY ABRAM

LETTER TO THE READER

Dear Reader,

I'm writing this letter to you because I've been where you are. I understand the daily frustration of being stuck in a position. I know the feeling of being unchallenged, under-appreciated, and passed over. I have witnessed others who I believed to be less qualified get promoted over and over. I've also been on the short end of the list when companies decided who to keep and who to let go during tough economic times. Or, similarly, not making the cut when it was time to hire again.

I spent years wondering, what is their secret. How do the "privileged few" seem to, not just land on their feet, but continue to move up the ladder toward the "C Suite"? True, hard work and persistence are part of the puzzle, and some seem to move up based on that alone. Keep doing a great job and someone will notice, right? However, there seemed to be some executives who seem to be hand-picked to drive in the fast lane, while you feel like you're stuck in a no-passing lane behind a garbage truck.

What is their secret? Why do they constantly get the hook-up? Is it because they come from privilege? The truth is that everyone and every situation is different. However, there are things you can do to "hack privilege."

In this book, I'll show you things you can do to increase your chances of getting on the fast track and finally getting what you want out of your career and your life.

This is a workbook with the emphasis on the word work. Yes, there is a lot of theory and scientific data presented, but it won't do you any good if you don't do the work. You will be challenged, you will be pushed out of your comfort zone, you will say to yourself, "I could never do that." Yet, if you follow the steps in this book, you will be transformed. All I can do is show you the way. You have to put in the work.

Within every chapter I will include several exercises for you to complete. You may not understand the purpose of every exercise, but do it anyway. When it all comes together, you will find yourself connecting with the types of people you want to have in your life, the types of people who can help take your career to the next level.

The "Connect Like A Boss" system is comprised of seven steps.

Deciding What You Want

Before you can get to where you think you want to be, you must first have a clear vision of what you want. What are your career goals? One of the worst things that can happen in your life is to spend years climbing a ladder only to realize you've been climbing the wrong ladder. Before we take one step, let's first get a clear understanding of your core values and make sure that your goals are aligned with them. We'll create the map BEFORE we start our journey.

Discovering Who You Are & How People See You

That sounds like a simple question, but in reality, most of us don't really know who we really are and even less about what others think about us. In this chapter, we talk about simple evaluation techniques like the Johari Window and the DISC Assessment.

Identifying Who You Need

Now that you have a better understanding of your goals and clarity on what success means to you, we can begin identifying the types of people you need in your network to help you get there. How does your current network look? Can you identify ten people who can directly help you achieve the things you decided on in the last chapter? If you want to be a Marketing Vice President, do you have the names of any Chief Marketing Officers in your rolodex? In this section, we'll create your Relationship Action Plan — a detailed list of the people you need to know and who you already know that can make introductions.

Being More Likable (Authentic, Generous, Friendly & Empathic)

People do business with, and promote, people that they like. What are some soft skills you can work on to become more likable? The keys to likability are Authenticity, Generosity, Trustworthiness and Empathy. Unfortunately, we are never taught these things in school. Conventional wisdom says that either you possess these skills or not. In this chapter we dive in to ways to develop each of those skills to become a more likable person.

Walk and Talk Like A Boss

Your self-talk can be the biggest booster or roadblock depending on the language you use when you talk to yourself. This chapter will show you how to erase the negative self-talk with positive, encouraging messages that will help you bring your best energy to interactions. People love to work with winners. Are you subconsciously projecting a winner's attitude? Do you stand, walk and talk like you are in command of your environment? I'll show you some techniques you can use to project confidence (even if you don't feel very courageous).

Working The Room Like A Boss

The bane of professional life is the networking event. Seen as a necessary evil by most, it is a must-do for career advancement. Where should you stand? How long should you talk to people? How do you start a conversation, and more importantly, how do you end one? What do you do if someone doesn't have a card? How to treat sweaty palms? These and other questions will be answered inside.

Following Up Like A Boss

Everything else is for naught if you don't get this part right. Ironically, this is where most people fail. Do you have a box of business cards somewhere in your house filled with business cards you have collected over the years yet you never contacted any of the people? How many of those contacts could introduce you to the people you need to know? Learn how to follow up and build relationships with the people who can help you systematically.

Who This Book Is For:

- Career business executives with 5+ years of experience
- Career business executives who are considering a move to entrepreneurship
- Career Academics who want to move up in their fields

Who This Book Is Not For:

- Students
- Solopreneurs (That's the next book)
- Politicians (Still another book)

TABLE OF CONTENT

INTRODUCTION

No, no, no, no, no. This cannot be happening again I thought as my manager announced the upcoming layoffs to a roomful of project managers. This had become a recurring theme in my life. And as I write these words, the feeling of absolute despair grips my stomach just as it did on that day in October of 2016. Every year over the previous four years, I had been called into a similar room and given the same news. Somehow, I had gotten onto this job roller coaster and couldn't figure out how to get off.

Somehow though, this time was different. The pain had become too great.The uncertainty too unbearable. Something had to change. Thus, I began my new journey. I've always been a believer that you could have anything you want out of life if you could just figure it out. If I'm not receiving the outcomes I'm expecting, I need to change something on my end.

After months of introspection, I concluded that my problem was an inability to connect with people. Sure, I knew people and had some friends, but at a fundamental level, I don't know them well and they really didn't know me. I had unknowingly put up a shell to protect myself. From what, I didn't know for sure, but I knew that I had to make a change in that area if I was going to get out of my rut.

So, I spent the next two years researching all of the physical and psychological aspects of connecting with people. I used to think I was studying networking. While networking is a part of the process, there is a distinct difference in networking and connecting. Networking is simply introducing yourself, which is important, but it is in connecting that everything flows.

In this book, I'll show you how true connection begins on the inside. Identifying who you are, what you want, and who can help you get there are the foundational aspects of building a strong network. You may believe that you are way too introverted to build a network. All your life you've grown to believe that you are too quiet, or too shy to make a lot of friends. Take it from me. After you have finished this book, you will have developed a skillset that you can use take your career to another level and Connect Like A Boss.

If you are reading this, you are likely somewhere on your career journey. You may be fresh out of school or a 20-year veteran. Whichever camp you're in, you're here because you aspire to have a better or different career. As you probably have realized by now, the key to getting ahead in your career is by having the right connections. You are ten times more likely to get a job through someone you know. You are also three times more likely to be successful in a position that comes through someone who knows you outside of work.

You may feel as if you have a pretty good network or you may identify as a certified wallflower. Either way, I guarantee you will find information in this book that can help you build a successful career. In the next several chapters, I will walk you step by step through the process of what I call "hacking privilege."

Privilege is generally granted by family connections. Some people have a parent or relative who can pick up the phone to give their career a boost. A little-known fact about Bill Gates is that his mother served on the executive board of the United Way with IBM CEO, John Opel. Do you think it was a coincidence that one of the largest companies in the world, IBM, tapped a nineteen-year-old college dropout to build the operating system for their new flagship product?

Since most of us don't have a family connection to a Fortune 500 CEO, we have to go about creating our own privilege by forming and developing our own high-level relationships. The problem is that most of us have no idea how to do that. It seems like it comes naturally to some people. The reality is that you can learn the strategies it takes to make your own connections by following the steps I'll lay out in this book.

In this book, I'll introduce you to the Seven Step

Connect Like A Boss Framework:

- Goal Setting
- Self-Awareness
- Identifying Your Circle
- Likability
- Leveling Up
- Working A Room
- Following Up

Goal Setting - This is where all starts. If you try to build a network without first identifying your goals, you'll end up wasting a lot of time going in the wrong direction. Here is where you identify your why and your core values. Skip this step at your own peril, and risk getting to the top of the wrong career for you.

Self-Awareness - Let's face it. The common denominator to all your relationships is Y.O.U. If you're not getting the jobs and promotions you think you deserve, it could be your personal brand. What do people say about you when you're not in the room? Do you have a blind spot? Let's find out.

Identifying Your Circle - If all of your jobs and career promotions come through people, doesn't it make sense to have the very best group of people in your circle? In this section, we identify the people you need in your circle and why. Then we break down some myths that may be preventing you from developing positive relationships with them.

Likability - Fair or not, people hire and promote people

that they like. The decision on whether someone likes you or not is made within the first thirty seconds. Quite often before you have even uttered a word. In this section we'll work on your "first impression," and how to increase your know-like-trust factor.

Leveling up - Winners like to work with other winners. If you want to be a part of the winner's circle, you have to think and act like one. You can adjust your self-talk and your executive presence to attract the attention of the people at the top of your organization. Connecting like a boss starts inside.

Working a room - The thought of walking into a room filled with strangers with the explicit intent of holding conversations with all of them strikes most people's hearts with terror. This section will give you strategies to work the room like a boss, and never succumb to that fear again.

Following up - A common misconception about building a network is that you need more contacts in order to be successful. The reality is that you have access to many contacts. As evidence, pull out that shoebox full of business cards that you have in your bedroom or office. The solution is having a system that you can use to keep in touch with people and stay top of their mind throughout their career.

CHAPTER ONE

DECIDING WHAT YOU WANT

"People may spend their whole lives climbing the ladder of success only to find, once they reach the top, that the ladder is leaning against the wrong wall." - Thomas Merton

———

The first step to Connecting Like A Boss and building the career you've dreamed of is first, knowing what you want. But what does that mean? Many of us go about our day-to-day activities thinking that we will "figure it out someday." This is like jumping in a car and driving for days with no clear idea what your destination is. Of course, no one would ever do that, so why do we take similar action with our lives? In this chapter, we will work on strategies that will help you decide what you really want out of life and create goals that will get you there.

I'm sure you are familiar with the story of King Midas. In this Greek legend, Midas, the king of Phrygia, did a favor for the god Dionysus. Dionysus was so pleased that he offered the king one wish. The story continues with Midas wishing that anything he touched would turn to gold. Unfortunately, he quickly realized his mistake when his dinner, mattress, and even his daughter were turned to solid gold. This is what happens when we get what we think we want without thinking it through. The strategies in this book will show you how to reach the level of career success that you want. However, before we get started, let's make sure you take some time to think about what you really want and why.

Like King Midas, many of us believe in more, better, and bigger. We are taught, almost from the cradle, that if we can make more money, drive a faster car, or live in a bigger house, then we will be happy. The strange thing is that even when we hear multiple stories in the news about people who have everything and are still unhappy, we still envy them. In his book, Super Rich, Russell Simmons recounts the story of his brother Joey "Run" Simmons' early days of living in a mansion. One afternoon while he was relaxing in the hot tub in his bedroom, he asked his butler to bring him a sandwich. As he sat in his hot tub eating his sandwich, it hit him. He had everything he could possibly want in the world, but he still wasn't happy. He had learned a hard lesson. All of the money in the world can't buy you one minute of joy.

Now I don't want you to think that there is something inherently wrong with money or being wealthy. Please feel free to get a rich as you want. Just don't think that the money alone will bring you happiness. What brings you happiness is becoming the person who deserves the money. One common misconception about goals is that they are about achieving something. That's incorrect. Goals are really about becoming the person you want to become. During the process of achieving your goals, you should actually become the type of person who deserves to have these possessions. Things don't come into your life simply because you want them; you have to put forth the effort to become the person who deserves them. The things you have in life are simply an echo of the effort you exert and the value you bring to the world.

What's Your Why?

When most people think of goals they think of them as What Do I Want? But the real question that needs to be asked is Why Do I Want It? The root of motivation is motive. If your motive is not based on becoming a better version of yourself, you may end up with a corner office, but what an empty feeling you will have if you don't feel like you deserve to be there. Like the body builder who takes illegal steroids or the pop singer who lip syncs, your win will seem hollow and you may even suffer from imposter syndrome, a state in which you live in constant fear of being found out. Many executives who moved up the ranks at their companies very quickly without accumulating the right experience and knowledge suffer from this daily.

Also, finding your why can serve as fuel for your career quest. Friedrich Nietzsche is quoted as saying, "I can accomplish any **How** as long as my **Why** is big enough." Understanding your own personal **why** is critical to long-term, career success.

I remember watching an interview with the most decorated Olympian of all time, Michael Phelps, in which he revealed his absolute hatred of early morning swims. He said, "Do you know how cold a swimming pool is at 5:30 am in the morning when you're the first one in it?" He hated it, but he fought through that pain every morning because his **why** around winning was so much stronger than his pain. Reaching big life goals is a process that requires a large amount of sacrifice and willpower. However, for the few that can attain the level of emotion needed to become a new person, success is on the horizon.

Here is a tool you can use to help you discover your **why** called the Five Whys Technique. Although it was developed in the 1930s by Sakichi Toyoda, the founder of Toyota, the company still uses it as a management technique today. Basically, you keep asking why until you get to the root of your purpose.

Here is an example below:

I want to get promoted to Vice President.

1. **Why do you want to be a Vice President?**

Because as Vice President, my ideas will get visibility.

2. Why is it important that your ideas get visibility?

Because if my ideas are visible, people will take action on them.

3. Why is it important that people take action on your ideas?

Because my ideas are better than some of the plans I've seen around here.

4. Why do you believe your ideas are better?

I don't know; I just believe it.

5. Why should you be promoted without any evidence?

Do you see what happened there? When you get to the root of your rationale, you may not have a very strong why. It doesn't mean that you shouldn't become vice president. It just means that you need to give more thought as to why it is really important to you. Use this technique to analyze your current goals to see if they still pass muster when you ask why.

When your Why is strong enough, you can experience the feeling that having a successful career will give you. Focus on your self-development, like Olympic athletes, to achieve goals. They spend years becoming the people who deserve the gold medal. When they step on that track or jump in that pool, they have the confidence of knowing they put in the work to become a champion. The emotion that comes along with that confidence is what gets them up every morning. You can use the same types of emotional attachment to drive the changes you need to become the person you need to be.

What Do You Truly Value?

Another method to deciding on a good career goal is to identify your core values. By discovering these values, you can make better decisions about the type of path you should be on. Are you in a career because of external forces like parents or school buddies? Do you think this career can bring you the most money?

Exercise: Take a look at the following list of common values and see if you can find words that resonate with you. Circle all that apply. Try not to choose more than 10-20 values from this list.

Core Values List Source scottjeffrey.com

Acceptance	Determination	Intelligence	Sharing
Accomplishment	Development	Intensity	Significance

Accountability	Devotion	Intuitive	Silence
Accuracy	Dignity	Joy	Simplicity
Achievement	Discipline	Justice	Sincerity
Adaptability	Discovery	Kindness	Skill
Alertness	Drive	Knowledge	Skillfulness
Altruism	Effectiveness	Leadership	Smart
Ambition	Efficiency	Learning	Solitude
Amusement	Empathy	Liberty	Spirit
Assertiveness	Empower	Logic	Spirituality
Attentive	Endurance	Love	Spontaneous
Awareness	Energy	Loyalty	Stability
Balance	Enjoyment	Mastery	Status
Beauty	Enthusiasm	Maturity	Stewardship

Boldness	Equality	Meaning	Strength
Bravery	Ethical	Moderation	Structure
Brilliance	Excellence	Motivation	Success
Calm	Experience	Openness	Support
Candor	Exploration	Optimism	Surprise
Capable	Expressive	Order	Sustainability
Careful	Fairness	Organization	Talent
Certainty	Family	Originality	Teamwork
Challenge	Famous	Passion	Temperance
Charity	Fearless	Patience	Thankful
Cleanliness	Feelings	Peace	Thorough
Clear	Ferocious	Performance	Thoughtful
Clever	Fidelity	Persistence	Timeliness
Comfort	Focus	Playfulness	Tolerance

Commitment	Foresight	Poise	Toughness
Common sense	Fortitude	Potential	Traditional
Communication	Freedom	Power	Tranquility
Community	Friendship	Present	Transparency
Compassion	Fun	Productivity	Trust
Competence	Generosity	Professionalism	Trustworthy
Concentration	Genius	Prosperity	Truth
Confidence	Giving	Purpose	Understanding
Connection	Goodness	Quality	Uniqueness
Consciousness	Grace	Realistic	Unity
Consistency	Gratitude	Reason	Valor
Contentmen	Greatness	Recognition	Victory

t			
Contribution	Growth	Recreation	Vigor
Control	Happiness	Reflective	Vision
Conviction	Hard work	Respect	Vitality
Cooperation	Harmony	Responsibility	Wealth
Courage	Health	Restraint	Welcoming
Courtesy	Honesty	Results-oriented	Winning
Creation	Honor	Reverence	Wisdom
Creativity	Hope	Rigor	Wonder
Credibility	Humility	Risk	
Curiosity	Humor	Satisfaction	
Decisive	Imagination	Security	
Decisiveness	Improvement	Self-reliance	
Dedication	Independence	Selfless	

Dependability	Individuality	Sensitivity	
Insightful	Innovation	Serenity	
Integrity	Inquisitive	Service	

Next, write out a list of all the words you wrote down or circled and begin to narrow it down to 5-10 core values. Because many of the words are very similar, you need a way prioritize which ones are MOST important. The best way to prioritize them is by comparing two at a time and thinking of a scenario in which you would have to choose between the two. For instance.Serenity and Peace are very similar, but mean slightly different things. Words are important. Crack open a dictionary and make sure you are being as specific as possible.

Of course, the importance of certain values will change based on the situation, but the more time you spend going through this exercise and refining your values, the more clearly you will know which ones make up your core set of unshakable values.

Another exercise I recommend is giving some thought to what it is that you are naturally really good at. I believe that we are all born with certain gifts and talents. I like to think that our time here on earth is for us simply to discover what they are and to help others using our innate skills.

As we discussed earlier in this chapter, in our society we place too much importance on things like money and status. However, anecdotal evidence shows that those who have achieved huge amounts of both are quite often the least happy among us. Your focus should be on the intersection of what you do well and what brings you joy, not what brings you the largest amount of possessions or greatest amount of money.

If you can successfully identify your why and your core values, you will be on your way to taking the first step towards authentic connection and true success.

You Need Goals That Line Up With Your Values

Now that you have identified your core values, you can create a list of goals that are in line with those values. This can help guide you in your career choice. If you value freedom, maybe a job that keeps you chained to a desk all day is not the one for you. Everyone's chart is different. It's up to you to define goals that resonate with your values. Now, when you practice goal setting you can be sure that reaching your goals will be meaningful and that you are becoming the person you need to be to achieve those goals.

A simple mnemonic tool I use when creating my goal's roadmap is to remember to PAVE the road. In order to achieve the success you seek, your goals must be:

P - Principle based. Your goals must align with your principles. What are your principles? Have you ever given it thought? If you're like most people, you believe you are a principled person. You know you have principles, but have never actually vocalized them or given language to them. Here's a thought experiment that can help you based on Stephen R. Covey's "Begin With The End In Mind" concept. Imagine you are at your own funeral. People get up one by one to say a few words. What do they say? Are there consistent themes? These are your principles. If the things being said about you are not aligned with what you want them to ultimately say, you still have time to fix that now.

A – Attainable. Can you see yourself ever achieving this goal? You've probably heard that anything you can conceive, you can achieve. The missing word in that sentence is believe. You also have to believe that you can attain the necessary skills and experience to achieve the goal. If you don't totally believe it, you will not have the perseverance to push through the tough times needed to cross the finish line. It's okay to pick big goals, but you must believe you can achieve them, even if you don't know how it is possible today.

V - Value Driven. Does this goal align with your core values? Everything you accomplish in life has to be aligned to your values. If you chase goals based on what you think others want for you, or what you think will impress people, you are doomed to a life of frustration.

It's much better to base your goals and ambitions on things that align with your values.

E - Exciting. Do you feel excited about your goal? If you don't feel excited about reaching the goal, the chance of you reaching it are greatly reduced. Pick goals that excite you. If you don't feel any strong emotions about a goal, then you have probably picked the wrong goal. The key to staying motivated through the tough times is to become emotionally attached to the outcome.

Exercise:

Write a list of 4-5 life goals in a column. In another column, write down the core value that aligns with the goal. If the goal does not align with your value, maybe you should rethink it.

Life Goal	Value

CHAPTER TWO

DISCOVERING WHO YOU ARE

True Connection Begins On The Inside

One of the worst pieces of advice I've ever heard was fake it until you make it. The platitude sounds good on the surface. The thought behind it is that you put on a facade of success until that success actually happens. Unfortunately, that rarely works. The fear of being found out as a phony can be debilitating and will actually work against what you are trying to accomplish.

American psychologist, Paul Elkman, whose theories were used as the basis for the hit TV show, "Lie To Me," discovered the concept of microexpressions. By using slow motion, video capture technology, he discovered that the human face constantly moves and contorts during conversations in an uncontrollable fashion. The science backs this up. When you hear or see something, that information is routed first to your limbic system which tells you how you feel about something before it hits your neocortex which tells you what you think about it. Since you have no conscious control over how you feel about something, your face reacts to those feelings, if only for a split second before you can "fix your face." While these expressions are not apparent to the person you are conversing with, the person will sense a lack of congruence between who you claim to be and who you actually are.

You've probably experienced this for yourself. That sense of something is not quite right about this person, I can't quite put a finger on it, but I just feel uncomfortable around them. If you are practicing the fake it until you make it strategy, it is likely that people feel the same about you. A better strategy is to identify the areas of uncertainty and fix them, while you are making it. And by doing that you will become a better version of yourself. Someone that others naturally gravitate towards.

Becoming the Real You

First, you have to wrap your head around the fact that the person you see in your mind's eye driving that Italian sports car, or walking on the marble floors of the multimillion dollar mansion is not you. That is a completely different person altogether. What blocks many people is that they want to remain the same and still have different things and experiences. However, it doesn't work that way. If you want to be an executive with a corner office, you must first become that executive on the inside.

Here is where you can put your imagination to work. Who is this person that you want to become? If you could magically put on a mask like a character in "Mission Impossible" who would you be? What characteristics does this person have? How does he or she treat people? Is he or she a good listener? How does this person dress? Is he or she punctual? But before you can become someone else, it is helpful to get a firm understanding of who you currently are and where you have to go.

Who Are You?

"No man ever steps in the same river twice, for it's not the same river and he's not the same man." - Heraclitus

According to Stanford researcher, Carol Dweck, people tend to have two different types of mindsets: a growth mindset and a fixed mindset. People with a fixed mindset believe that they were born with a certain set of abilities and limitations. If you frequently hear yourself saying, "That's just how I am" or "I've always been this way," you are displaying fixed mindset tendencies. On the other hand, people with a growth mindset believe that they can learn and grow throughout their lives. They believe that their abilities can be developed and improved through dedication and hard work.

The fixed mindset is easier to have and, therefore, more common than growth mindset. But it's important to develop a growth mindset to connect like a boss. otherwise you won't exert the required effort and you will remain stuck. Adopting a growth mindset is simply about understanding that if there is something about yourself that you want to improve, you can do it. You just have to put in the work.

When most people think of improving themselves, they think about physical enhancements. However, like I said earlier, change starts on the inside, and another word for your inside is your personality. You may be thinking that your personality is pretty hard-boiled and cannot be changed. Remember the growth mindset? You can change almost any element of yourself including your personality if you're willing to do the work.

The first step to improving your personality is understanding what your personality type is. If someone asked you to describe yourself, you would most likely start with your height, weight, hair color, etc. However, if the request was to describe your personality you would probably struggle to nail down details.

One good way to look at your personality objectively is by using the Five Factor Model. Developed by Robert McCrae and Paul Costa in 1986, a subject is asked to read a number of descriptions or adjectives and to rate the accuracy with which they describe their own personality on a Likert scale. At the end of the exercise. the subject will have a clearer understanding of where they fall on the dimensions listed below, and can use that data to work on areas of their personality that may be holding them back from their career goals.

Take a look at the five items below and then use the likert scale that follows to help define your personality type. You will also be able to use this scale to quickly identify your colleagues and adjust your communication with them.

1. Openness to Experience

The openness dimension is characterized by a willingness to try new activities. People with higher levels of openness will listen to unconventional ideas and beliefs. They are also more likely to accept ideas that they initially disagreed with.

They tend to enjoy artistic and cultural experiences. They are also more open to unfamiliar cultures and customs.

People with low levels of openness avoid areas of uncertainty and the unknown. They are less willing to accept beliefs and ideas which challenge the status quo.

Less open individuals feel uncomfortable in unfamiliar situations and prefer familiar environments. They value the safety of predictability, and stick to well-known traditions and routines.

2. Conscientiousness

Conscientious people are very aware of the consequences of their actions. They feel a sense of responsibility for others, and are generally careful to live up to expectations. Conscientious individuals are punctual, tidy and well-organized.

Highly conscientious people are also very goal-oriented. They set ambitious goals and work hard to achieve them. They are keen to succeed in every aspect of their lives.

Low conscientiousness levels result in less motivated behavior. Unconscientious individuals are less concerned by tidiness and punctuality. This group of people arrives late to meetings and is less motivated to achieve life goals. They also engage in impulsive behavior without considering the consequences of their choices.

3. Extroversion

Extroverts are outgoing and confident in social settings. They enjoy being the center of a group, and will often seek the attention of others. They love meeting new people, and are happy to introduce themselves to strangers. They thrive in group settings.

People with low levels of extraversion often appear shy around other people. They feel uncomfortable in large groups, and will often avoid large social gatherings.

Introverts enjoy being a part of smaller social groups, with familiar people. They tend to maintain a close group of trusted friends.

4. Agreeableness

If you are an agreeable person, you are likely to be seen as friendly, and more likeable by your peers. Agreeable people are trusting of others and willing to help during times of need. Their ability to work with others means that they often work well as members of a team.

Agreeable people dislike arguments or any type of confrontation. They seek to appease others, acting as the mediating peacemaker of their group.

People who are disagreeable are less concerned with pleasing people or making friends. Disagreeable people are more suspicious of people's intentions, and are less charitable.

They tend to act in their own self-interest, showing less regard for the needs of others. As a result, others see them as being selfish rather than agreeable.

5. Neuroticism

This dimension ranges from emotional stability to emotional instability or neuroticism. People with high neuroticism scores are often persistent worriers. They are more fearful and anxious. They overthink their problems and blow things out of proportion. Neurotic people tend to overstate the negative implications of a situation. They become frustrated with others and may feel angry if events do not occur as they wish.

People with low neuroticism scores are less preoccupied by these negative concerns. They are able to remain calm in stressful situations. As a result, they tend to worry less about such problems.

Exercise: Use the chart below to circle where you think you are on this scale based on the information above.

Openness To Experience

Low 1 2 3 4 5 6 7 8 9 High

Conscientiousness

Low 1 2 3 4 5 6 7 8 9 High

Extraversion

Low 1 2 3 4 5 6 7 8 9 High

Agreeableness

Low 1 2 3 4 5 6 7 8 9 High

Neuroticism

Low 1 2 3 4 5 6 7 8 9 High

What did this reveal? Does your stated career goal line up with your personality type? For example, do you want to be a sales manager, but your Agreeableness and Openness scores are both one? Were you looking into the medical profession, but found out you're not very conscientious? If your scores don't align with your goals, you have two choices: you can either adjust your goals based on these findings or you can adopt a growth mindset to adjust the levels of these scores. Obviously, changing your personality will take some work, and is outside of the scope of this book. However, it can be done.

The DISC assessment

If you are looking for a more objective take on your personality, there is a tool called the DISC assessment. The acronym DISC stands for Dominance, Influence, Steadiness and Conscientiousness. To get your profile, you go online and answer a series of questions – Tony Robbins provides a free version on his website https://www.tonyrobbins.com/disc/. The software then calculates which parts of your personality are stronger. If you are Dominant, you place more emphasis on accomplishing results, you're focused on the bottom line and you are seen as being very confident. If you are an Influencer, you place more emphasis on persuading others, and building relationships. If you are Steady, you emphasizes cooperation, and dependability. And if you are Conscientious, you focus on quality and like to be seen as competent.

When you take this test, it will be eye opening, and you may have some surprises in store.

The Johari Window

Another tool that is very effective at addressing the awareness problem is the Johari Window. Created in 1955 by psychologists, Joseph Luft and Harrington Ingham, the Johari Window is an exercise that helps people identify blind spots and areas of improvement. In the exercise, a person is given a list of fifty-six adjectives like dependable, confident, helpful etc. and they are asked to select the words they feel best describe their personality. That same list is then given to the person's peers. The peers don't know what the person has already selected. The peers then select the words they think best describe the person.

Words that are selected by both subject and their peers go in the top left quadrant. Words that are select by peers, but not by the subject go in the top right. Words that are selected by the subject, but not by the peers are considered hidden or a façade, and go in the bottom left. The rest of the words go in the bottom right, Unknown.

Johari Window

	Known to self	Not known to self
Known to others		
	Arena	Blind Spot
Not Known to Others		
	Façade	Unknown

The key to the exercise is to look at the list and decide which words that you want applied to you. Those words should appear in the Arena, or top left quadrant. Next, you need to understand your blind spots. Did this exercise reveal anything that you were totally unaware of? Do people think you are confident when you feel unsure or is the opposite true. If you're like most people you will have some work to do in this area.

One part of this chart that I find fascinating is the Façade—the things that you know about yourself that others can't see. Are there things you can do to highlight these areas? Make sure you try this exercise out for yourself. There are some online tools that should be fairly easy to find so that you can conduct the test for yourself. I recommend using the free version found at https://kevan.org/johari .

CHAPTER THREE

IDENTIFYING WHO YOU NEED

If you want to go fast, go alone. If you want to go far, go together. **- African Proverb**

───────

Now that you have identified what you want, and more importantly, why you want those goals, you can begin to identify the types of people you need to have in your life to take you there. What I'm going to cover in this chapter is what your network should look like, how many people you should have in your network and how do you decide who's in and who's out.

When I was younger, I enjoyed playing video games. The basic concept of one game was that the lead character would be given some seemingly impossible mission to accomplish. Along his journey, he would meet various people, and make a judgment call as to whether this person would be an asset or a liability, a friend or an enemy. He relied mainly on his gut instincts, and sometimes he had intel from his command post. The key takeaway from the game was even though he was alone during the mission, he couldn't be successful without the help of others. As you go about your career journey, how do you know who can help you get where you are trying to go from who will hold you back?

Acquiring this skill is going to be key to building the type of network that can help take your career to the next level. The people you have in your circle will either propel you to the next level or hold you back from your dreams. For instance, you may have heard that your net income is the average of your five closest friends. Think of the people in your life as your team. If, like in a game of pickup basketball, you picked the best forward, center and guard available, you could stack the odds and make sure you won almost every game you played. The good news is that you can do that in your work life as well. You just have to think about your friendships, and relationships a bit differently.

Create Your People Plan

If you have ever had your own business or have run a team for a company, chances are you created a business plan showing the strategy and demographics for the business. Likewise, you have probably created a budget or financial plan of some type. However, you've probably never created a "people plan."

A people plan is simply a list of people who can help you reach your goals. As you may realize, everything you have or want to have, comes from or through people. Wouldn't it make sense to have the people in your life who can help you get the things you want? Yet, surprisingly, that's not how most of us operate. We accumulate contacts and connections with little forethought whatsoever. The results are the same as building a house with no blueprint. You won't get the results you're after.

Of course, everyone in your life is not going to be a direct connection to one of your goals. However, if you look through your current contact list, and don't see many people who can help you advance, you will need to reassess your contacts. Researcher Mark Granovetter, in his book, Getting A Job, discovered during his research that the number one indicator of career success was a person's self-identified peer group. Basically, if your peers are high achievers, then you likely will be a high-achiever yourself.

You may ask, where do I start? You can start right where you are, with who you already know. Think about all of the people you have listed in your phone, and the people whose names you have collected over the years. How many people do you communicate with regularly? If you're like most people, you talk to the same five to ten people over and over. This is your comfort zone. People that you are comfortable talking with, people who understand you. We all have those people in our lives, but in order to get your career where you want it to go, you are going to have to expand your horizons, and break out of your comfort zone.

The first step is to clean up your contact list. If you are like most people, you have simply collected names and numbers from your various jobs, conferences and travels over the years. Many of these contacts haven't been called in years and some have never been called at all. So, the first step is to contact everyone in your phone. This may sound like a big, unpleasant job. However, once you start you will be pleasantly surprised at how people respond. Most people are conditioned to believe that the only people who call them are people who want something. So, when you call just to say hello, with no agenda, they will be glad to hear from you. Now you can have a normal conversation and ask about how things are going for them.

Here's what this exercise accomplishes. It allows you to quickly see which numbers are no longer valid, who you don't remember and who doesn't remember you. Those numbers you can delete. Also, if you see a name and you get a bad feeling about calling them, you can delete those too. What you have also done at the end of this exercise is find out what people are working on as well as letting them know what you are working on. Again, it is important that you don't have an agenda for this call. Nothing is a bigger turnoff than to get a call from someone you haven't heard from in years asking for a job. Conversely, there is no bigger turn on then someone calling you who is genuinely interested with your well-being and current activities.

The goal here is simply to re-establish a connection. Once, that is done you can begin setting up your organizational structure for your contacts. I use something called the ABCD structure to organize my contacts.

A- Ambassador: These are the people who know your work and abilities and will always recommend you for jobs. These are quite often good friends or family members. However, they can be people who you are not particularly close with, but who believe in you and your abilities.

B - Business Associate: These are people who you do business with. They may be a customer of yours or you may be a customer of theirs. This group is also reserved for co-workers and organization members.

C - Comforter: These are the people that we call most frequently. The person you think to call when something very good or something very bad happens to us. These are the people that we spend 80-90% of our time talking too.

D- Delete: These are the people that we should not have in our lives. If someone has poor energy or has shown you that they will not help you, remove them from your list of contacts.

For the next exercise, create a grid like the one below. Try to list everyone in your current list of contacts. If you have a lot of names, it will seem like a big job, but it's so worth it at the end. Remember, you are only listing the names of people that you want to remain in contact with. To prevent having to write it all down by hand, most contact systems will allow you to export to Excel.

Once you have your list, mark next to each name whether the person is an A, B or C. Then in the next column write a one-word description of how your current relationship is with them. If your relationship is poor or broken, you can work on improving the relationship with that person.

Name	ABCD	Relationship	
Joe Brown	A	Good	
Tasha St. Patrick	B	Poor	
Tom David son	A	Good	
Tricia Stevens	C	Broken	

In future chapters, I will walk you through how to build better relationships with contacts that you don't have a good relationship with right now and show you have to stay top-of-mind with the contacts that you already have a good relationship with. What we've accomplished here is a baseline so that you will know where you are in your networking journey. I find this exercise to be extremely eye opening. And many of my clients say that simply doing this exercise was completely life changing for them.

Now that you have an inventory of who is in your circle, and what your relationship is with them, you will figure out where you have gaps and fill them.

New Contacts

The approach I use to adding people to my network is the same as I use for adding friends to my life. I believe that there is value to being a part of my network, and I evaluate everyone who is in it, as well as anyone I am considering adding before I do.

Before we start adding people to your network, it's important that I dispel a few myths.

Myth #1 - Your work friends and your personal friends have to be different people. Why do you believe this is true? Are you concerned that if people found out about your real life they wouldn't like you anymore? Your fears are probably overrated. As long as you are living true to yourself, what difference does it make how you live your personal life. Also, like Dr. Phil says, "If you know how little time people spent thinking about you, it would totally change the way you approached life."

Myth #2 - You have nothing to offer the types of people, like senior executives, you want to add to your network. Nothing could be further from the truth. Everybody needs something. Your job is to figure out what that is and how you can provide it. You would be surprised that it is a simple as having a listening, non-judgmental ear.

Now that we have dispelled these myths let's get to work.

One of the biggest challenges people face when building their network is getting spread too thin. They join multiple groups, attend this event and the other with no focus on their goals. The key to being effective in your networking efforts is to make sure you are connecting with the people you need to connect with.

First, you must narrow down what type of people that you want to have in your network. That's right, you can decide in advance the types of people that you want to have in your network before you even begin introducing yourself to people. A great exercise for identifying the people you need in your network comes from the marketing world. In order to make sure that a product or marketing campaign is being developed for the proper customer, the marketing company creates something called a persona.

A persona is simply a document that is used to describe the ideal customer for the product that is being built or advertised. You can also use the same technique to narrow you refocus on the types of people who can be most helpful to you and your career.

When a persona is done well, it will contain a name and picture of the person, their income, likes, dislikes, education, family life, reading materials etc. The more details, the better. This exercise helps you decide who should be added to your circle and who should be removed.

This persona doesn't have to exist in your life now. Your persona may be the CEO of a Fortune 500 company, or CMO of a tech company. The only limits to your personas are your imagination. However, keep in mind the lessons from Chapter One. When you meet that person, make sure you have worked on becoming the type of person this new contact will want to be involved with.

As you are building your personas, keep in mind the traits of someone that you want to be in your circle. Remember, the people in your network represent you (birds of a feather). So, you must make sure that they are aligned with your core values.

CHAPTER FOUR

BEING MORE LIKEABLE

People may not remember what you say, or even what you do. They will, however, remember how you made them feel. - Maya Angelou

―――――

Think about someone in your life that you really like. Who is that person who brings a smile to your face as soon as they walk into the room? Chances are you feel some kind of connection with them. These types of connections are generally based on time or shared experience. Or are they? What are the factors that make you gravitate towards some people and not others? And can you replicate those characteristics in your own life so that people feel that way about you when you walk in the room?

Being seen as likeable is important because the entire reason for building a network and connecting with people is to surround ourselves with people who are more likely to say yes to your request. And we all know that people prefer to say yes to those that they like.

But what causes one person to like another? According to Robert Cialdini in his book, Influence, there are three important factors: we like people who are similar to us, who pay us compliments, and who help us reach mutual goals.

In conjunction with tapping into similarities and offering compliments, there are four characteristics that you need to develop to help people like you: Authenticity, Generosity, Trustworthiness, and Empathy. Each one of these traits is powerful, and in this chapter, you will learn how to understand and develop these characteristics to make your connections become stronger more quickly.

Authenticity

The first characteristic needed for true connection is authenticity. The ability to be true to yourself in all situations is also perhaps one of the hardest things for most of us to do. Especially at work. You would be mortified if your co-workers found out you still have a doll collection or that you own seventeen cats or that you grew up in a trailer home or whatever that thing is that makes you feel ashamed deep inside. Ironically, it is those very types of things that allow us to really connect with people.

For many of us, our self-esteem is based on what others think of us. We feel as if we are not worthy of acceptance just as we are. Here is a simple truth that you may not have heard recently, if ever. **You are enough**. So, get rid of the thought that you are not tall enough, pretty enough, skinny enough, smart enough to move ahead. I will say it again. **You are enough**. Just… as… you… are.

According to researcher, Brené Brown, in her book Daring Greatly, people create and wear a coat of armor that they carry around with them everywhere to shield themselves from anyone finding out their hidden shames (remember Johari's Window?). However, in doing so, they don't realize how much energy it consumes to keep up that facade. They believe, wrongly, that if they can protect themselves from shame and embarrassment, their lives will be easier. They believe that by showing up and letting themselves be seen, they are at risk of exposing themselves to the things they have spent their lives hiding from others. True, there is some risk, but the rewards are much greater than the cost.

Think about a time in your past when you tried to fit in with a group that really wasn't "you." Maybe you tried to fit in with the cool kids or the smart kids or the jocks. As Dr. Phil would say, "How did that work out for ya?" My guess is probably not so good. The problem with "fitting in" is that by not being true to yourself, you are telling a lie and we learned in previous chapters why that doesn't work. You cannot successfully connect with someone's similarities if your similarities are not true.

It is great to join other groups, but much better to do so on your own terms. People will actually appreciate honest feedback more than you going along with the group. For example, if your team goes to a movie and you didn't like it even though everyone else seemed to enjoy it, do you say you like it too or do you disagree? The easy choice is to go along with the group, but the more authentic choice is to speak your mind. Be mindful, however, that being authentic is not an excuse to be rude or unkind.

According to Dr. Brown, belonging to a group is one of the things that makes us human. The desire to belong is so strong that we mute ourselves in order to be a part of certain groups. What we don't realize is that this "fitting in" actually blocks us from ever actually belonging to that group. If they can't accept you for who you truly are, then it's better for you to find another group.

How To Be More Authentic

Give yourself permission to show up fully, as yourself. Remember back in grade school when your teacher would give you a permission slip to take home for your parent or guardian to sign? Well, now you are the adult and you have the power sign your own note. Take out a piece of paper and write "Today I give myself permission to be Me" and sign it. Put your note in your wallet or purse and use it as a reminder to just be yourself when faced with situations where you would have just "fit in" in the past.

Make truth telling a habit. One of my favorite movies is "Napoleon Dynamite." In an attempt to make himself more popular, he told grandiose lies.

Don: Hey, Napoleon. What did you do last summer again

Napoleon Dynamite: I told you! I spent it with my uncle in Alaska hunting wolverines!

Don: Did you shoot any

Napoleon Dynamite: Yes, like 50 of 'em! They kept trying to attack my cousins. What the heck would you do in a situation like that

Don: What kind of gun did you use?

Napoleon Dynamite: A freakin' 12-gauge, what do you think?

This scene is funny because everyone knows it's not true. But when you expand on your accomplishments to impress someone else, aren't you doing the same thing? While you may think of them as harmless white lies, people usually see through your camouflage making it more difficult for them to connect with the real you. When you speak your truth, authentically, you show others that you are responsible, that you can be trusted, and that you trust others enough to show your genuine, vulnerable self.

Generosity

Another characteristic to connect with someone is to

show them that you understand their needs and are happy to help them. One reality about being human is that everyone has something they need and everyone has something to offer. The entire nature of relationship building is based on the ability to find where these two meet for mutual benefit.

How do you determine what someone needs? Common wisdom suggests that you just ask directly. Have you ever ended a conversation with someone and they asked you, "Is there anything I can help you with?" How could you answer that question? "Yeah, I could use a hundred bucks if you don't mind"? I say that with tongue in cheek, but it's a real dilemma. Most of the time people don't know specifically what they need or if you would be the right person to help them.

A better way to gather the information is in a roundabout way that doesn't put either of you on the spot. For example, "What project has your focus right now? Are there any sticking points that you could use help with to get it completed?" Another good question is: "Do you have everything you need to hit your targets for this quarter?" Do you see how these questions could get someone to volunteer specific information about what they could specifically use help with without you preemptively volunteering to help?

There is no right or wrong way to be generous. You have to be creative and understand which of your unique gifts is a match for what the person you are connecting with needs. Many people mistakenly believe that generosity means spending money. That's not necessarily true. There are several ways that you can offer value without spending a die.

Connections

One of the greatest benefits to building a strong network is that you will have the ability to connect people to each other. Now when someone says they need help in a certain area, you can be forthcoming with a contact that could help them.

Opportunities

Whenever you learn about new opportunities, you can forward them to the people in your list. To magnify this effect, when you find out one of your contacts has a particular interest, you can set a Google alert for it. That way whenever something interesting pops up in your Inbox, you can forward it.

Articles

Similarly, as you scroll through your feed, keep an eye out for articles or blog posts on LinkedIn or your news feed that may be of interest to your connections. One of the great things about the internet today is that almost everything is shareable. Make sure you send them directly instead of just posting them to you network. That way the person you have in mind will know that you are thinking of them.

You may be asking at this point what is the purpose of these small favors, especially done for strangers or near strangers. In his book, 7 Habits of Highly Successful People, Stephen R. Covey talks about something called an emotional bank account. Your emotional back account works similarly to a regular bank where you make deposits and withdrawals, however your currency is kindness and requests. Every time you perform a kindness for someone, you are making a deposit and every time you make a request of someone you are making a withdrawal. By being generous, you are making sure you have currency in the emotional bank before you make a withdrawal.

In his book, Influence, Robert Cialdini calls this the Law Of Reciprocity. What Dr. Cialdini discovered in his research was that when you do a favor for someone, they will feel obligated to pay you back in some way. The important factor in this approach is to make sure your action or gift is seen as a kindness. You don't want to give a McDonald's gift certificate to a vegan, for instance.

One interesting quirk in this law is that you also have to make withdrawals from time to time. The reason is people like to help people who they have helped before. This is called The Benjamin Franklin effect. The story goes that when Franklin was running for the legislature, a peer chose to run against him and gave a long speech listing all of the reasons why no one in their right mind would vote for a scoundrel like Ben Franklin. While Franklin eventually won the election, he was quite upset that someone he knew would spend so much effort to troll him. Since this person was very wealthy and held significant sway in the local government, Franklin thought it better to turn him into a friend than an enemy.

So, Franklin set out to turn his hater into a fan, but he wanted to do it without ingratiating himself. Franklin sent a letter to the hater asking if he could borrow a specific selection from his library, one that was a "very scarce and curious book." The rival, flattered, sent it right away. Franklin sent it back a week later with a thank-you note. Mission accomplished. The next time the legislature met, the man approached Franklin and spoke to him in person for the first time. Franklin wrote that "he and the man became great friends, and their friendship continued to his death."

This story shows that generosity works both ways. You have to not only be willing to give value, you must also be willing to accept value from others.

Trustworthiness

A common myth about trustworthiness is that either you trust somebody or you don't. Once someone has decided that they don't trust you for whatever reason, that opinion is set in stone and there is nothing that can be done. I strongly disagree with this sentiment. Trust is something, like so many other aspects of relationships, that can be nurtured and grown if you know the right way to proceed.

It's imperative, that you understand what trust is. When most people think of trust, they believe it is a response to a person's integrity and character. However, there is another important factor that you take into consideration before deciding whether to trust someone. Before entering into a trusted relationship with anyone, ask yourself: "Do I believe this person is competent?" I have friends that I would trust to pay back a loan or borrow my car or even watch my house while I'm away on vacation. However, I wouldn't necessarily trust those friends to invest my money, repair my car or put a new roof on my house.

The concept of competence goes hand in hand with character, and in many ways is just as important. According to Stephen M. R. Covey in his book, The Speed Of Trust, character is a constant; it's necessary for trust in any circumstance. Competence, however, is situational; it depends on what the circumstance requires. Once you become aware that both character and competence are vital to trust, you can see how the combination of these two dimensions is reflected in the approach of effective leaders and connectors everywhere.

Like most of the other topics in this book, trust also begins inside. No one can trust you, more than you trust yourself. I'll say that again. No one can trust you more than you trust yourself. At this point, you may be thinking, "Of course I trust myself." I would challenge that assumption. Think about your New Year's resolutions. Did you accomplish them? How often have you made a commitment to yourself and then broken it? Conventional wisdom says that it's okay to break commitments to yourself because no one get hurt but you. I disagree.

Commitment is like a muscle and falls in line with being congruent in thought and deed. If you are not practiced at keeping commitments to yourself, you are less likely to keep commitments to others. As you let that sink in, think about some times in your life that you didn't accomplish something that you committed to, if only to yourself. Moving forward, don't let that happen again. Work diligently on keeping your commitments. The difference this will make to your life will be outstanding. Not only will you make necessary improvements in your own life, you will find that others trust you more and more.

Empathy

Empathy is the act of putting yourself in someone else's shoes. In order to be a good friend, you have to be able to listen, non-judgmentally, to what others are dealing with. One of the hardest parts about showing empathy is that sometimes you can't help. In some situations, the best course of action is simply to listen. Dr. Brown says that when we see a friend sitting in a dark room, our first instinct is to turn on the light. However, sometimes the friend just need somebody to sit in the dark with them for a little while.

Listening is the first step to connecting and finding similarities. All problems cannot be solved, but a listening ear offered, authentically, can build trust that can serve your relationship well over the years.

In a series of negotiation studies carried out between two groups of MBA students, one group was told, "Time is money. Get straight down to business." In this group, around fifty-five percent were able to come to an agreement.

A second group, however, was told, "Before you begin negotiating, exchange some personal information with each other. Identify a similarity you share in common then begin negotiating." In this group, ninety percent of them were able to come to successful and agreeable outcomes that were typically worth eighteen percent more to both parties.

As stated earlier, executives like to promote people they know, like and trust. We've talked about getting people to like and trust you. Now let's pull it all together into one package known as your presence.

Exercises

1. Share something personal with a colleague that you've never shared before. (Nothing so horrible that would make them wonder if they should call the police). Something that is relatively mundane, but might allow them to connect with you at a deeper level. For example, a hobby, or a favorite place you've visited.

2. Work on keeping commitments to yourself. People can trust you if you don't trust yourself. Try to make a small commitment and keep it no matter what. For example: I'll do 10 pushups every morning when I first wake up for a week. When you have success with that set another commitment and adhere to it.

3. Ask someone you don't know very well for a small favor. The act of them doing you a favor will help make them feel more connected to you and counterintuitively make them want to help you in the future.

CHAPTER FIVE

WALK AND TALK LIKE A BOSS

The past is history, tomorrow is a mystery today is a present. - Bill Kean

---

Neil Gaiman, author of several bestsellers, including American Gods, recounts a story that happened long after he had received dozens of awards and accolades. "Some years ago, I was lucky enough to be invited to a gathering of great artists and scientists, writers and explorers. I felt that at any moment they would realize that I didn't qualify to be there, among these people who had really done things. On my second night there, I was standing at the back of the hall, and I started talking to a very nice, polite, elderly gentleman about several things, including our shared first name. And then he pointed to the hall of people, and said, 'I just look at all these people, and I think, what the heck am I doing here? They've made amazing things. I just went where I was sent.' And I said, 'Yes. But you were the first man on the moon. I think that counts for something.' And I felt a bit better. Because if Neil Armstrong felt like an imposter, maybe everyone did."

Imposter Syndrome is the feeling in your gut that everyone in the meeting or event is smarter or at least more informed then you are. That feeling prevents you from speaking up because you are afraid of saying something stupid. This syndrome is so paralyzing because it prevents you from being your best self in the moment. At its core, overcoming imposter syndrome is what Connecting Like A Boss is all about.

When you believe you should be in the room and you are bringing your unique perspective and knowledge to the conversation, you begin to take on winning characteristics in other's minds. Another word for boss is winner. People like to work with winners. If I want my company, department, or team to be successful, I want as many winners as I can get. But being a winner does not necessarily mean being aggressive. Being a winner is about remaining calm and congruent no matter the situation. It's also about believing that you deserve to be in the room.

How To Be Seen As A Winner

How do you quiet the voice in your head telling you that you don't belong here, that voice that summons the paralyzing fear which prevents you from tapping into your personal power? How do you summon the quiet confidence of a winner? The key is being present. But what does that mean exactly?

According to Harvard Professor Amy Cuddy, being present is about narrating your own story. It's the ability to stop worrying about the impression you are making on others and focusing on the impression you are making on yourself. When you can make an honest internal connection with yourself, you have the power to be fully present. Then you can be fully congruent in thought, word and deed. As we talked about earlier, if your mouth is saying one thing, but your face says another, you will not be believable.

When you are fully congruent about why you deserve to be in the room, you will project that confidence externally. Here are some techniques I use to project a winning presence.

Look, Listen & Breathe

1. Look - Eye contact is one of the most effective ways of communicating non-verbally and establishing presence. You should establish and keep eye contact without getting into a staring contest. One trick I use to maintain eye contact without making the other person feel uncomfortable is what I call the triangle gaze. Look at their left eye for three seconds, then look at their right eye for three seconds, then look down at their mouth for three seconds. Repeat. Doing this gives the impression of focused eye contact without being creepy.

2. Listen - Active listening is critical to presence. When you listen, I mean really listen, you make a person feel

heard and valued. In return they will see you as a leader. Here's how to do it. Do not interrupt while the other person is speaking and do not prepare your reply while the other person speaks. Ask questions and paraphrase their last comment. "So, what I heard you say was" is a great way to show you are listening as well as giving them an opportunity to clarify. Bonus tip: Tilt your head a little to the right. It signals that you are interested in what they are saying.

3. Breathe - Simply remember to breathe. Breathing intentionally connects you to the present moment. It is very difficult for your mind to wander when you are connected to your breathing. As you are listening remember to breathe consciously. No need to make a big production out of it, but make sure you are pulling air all the way down into your diaphragm. In the activities section, I'll give you some breathing exercises you can use to empower your day and help you keep a winning mindset even when you don't particularly feel like a winner.

SELF TALK

Several years ago, a young lady visited her doctor. She said, "Doc, you've got to help me. Every time I eat strawberries I break out in a terrible rash." The doctor calmly replied, "Ok, let's have a look at you." After completing his exam, he pulled out his prescription pad and began scribbling. He handed the lady the prescription and, although the writing was horrible, she could make out the words. Stop Eating Strawberries.

While that story is told with tongue firmly in cheek, it resonates with many people because we are all guilty of self-inflicted pain. For instance, have you ever had a bruise? One of the properties of bruising is that it usually doesn't hurt at all until we touch it. Yet, what do we do all day? Touch it. Sounds ridiculous, but it's true.

What is worse is that we do the same things with our minds. If you're like most people, your memories are filled with dozens of "mental bruises." Things people said or did to you in the past that continue to cause you pain every time you revisit them. These memories only serve to limit you.

As Eckhart Tolle says in his book, The Power Of Now, "the inability to stop thinking is a terrible affliction." You may find that quote to be quite strange. You may think to yourself, "Of course I can stop thinking if I wanted to." Oh, really? I dare you to try to not think about anything for two minutes. Go ahead, I'll wait. I can already tell you how that ended. Unless you are a trained yogi, your mind is filled with incessant chatter, chatter that prevents you from ever being fully present.

Your mind is constantly commenting on everything, almost like you have a second head sticking out of your neck. A key question to ask yourself as you establish greater presence is who is in control, you or your mind? If you think you and your mind are one, I would beg to differ. When you talk to yourself, who is talking, and who is listening? If you are not sure, it's probably your mind. To misquote an old UNCF commercial: "The mind is a terrible thing." Of course, properly used, the mind is a great tool for thinking through problems. However, the mind usually serves as background noise that plays blasts from the past or visions of the future. Neither soundtrack serves you very well in the present.

Try A Little CBT

CBT, not CBD, is short for Cognitive Behavioral Therapy. This very complicated sounding term is actually a simple set of techniques that can help you overcome things like Imposter Syndrome and a dozen other mental roadblocks that can keep you from showing up as your best self. One very simple CBT technique you can start using today is called the Thought Bubble. If you have ever read a cartoon or comic book, you are familiar with thought bubbles. Draw a stick figure with a thought bubble. Now imagine a challenging situation at work, and fill in what you would be thinking.

The act of taking it out of your head can help you quite a bit as you try to understand why you feel that way. With time and practice you can even change the words in that bubble to more positive, empowering phrases. This is where affirmations come in handy.

Affirmations

One common misconception about affirmations is that they can change what you believe about yourself. In truth, successful affirmations serve as more of a reminder of who you are. You can tell yourself, "I am a millionaire" a million times, but it probably won't come true because you don't believe it. A better use of affirmations is to use the core values you identified in Chapter One. "I am (insert your core values here)" will resonate stronger and help you leverage your personal power so that when you are going into that big meeting or important event you can be reminded of your unique special gift you are bringing to the table.

Activities:

Short circuit your negative self-talk with reframing. Create a grid listing out several challenging situations at work and imagine what thoughts would pop into your head.

Situation	Thought	Reframe
Called into managers office	I must've messed something up	She probably needs my input on something
Typo in your presentation	I'm such a screw up. I can't do anything right	That's not good. I'll need to doublecheck next time
Group discussion	Nobody wants to hear my dumb idea	My feedback is important and valuable.

This list can be as long as you want to make it. The goal is to get in front of common situations and reframe your self-talk into something more positive.

Exercises

1. Calm yourself with your breath. The Navy Seals use something called Box Breathing before missions to help calm their nerves. Simply breath in for a count of four. Hold your breath for a count of four and then slowly exhale for a count of four. Try it now. You will see how, after a couple of repitiions, your brain and body begin to relax.

2. Create an accomplishment list. One reason why our self-talk can be so negative is because our brains tend to remember negative events more strongly than the positive ones. This is because the negative events can sometimes actually hurt us, and our brains are wired first to protect us from harm so anything that caused us either physical or emotional pain is very easily called into our remembrance. One way to combat this is by taking a piece of paper and writing down all of your accomplishments. Nothing is too far back or too trivial; if it made you smile it goes on the paper. I bet the list is a lot longer than you thought it would be.

CHAPTER SIX

WORK THE ROOM LIKE A BOSS

Nothing ventured nothing gained. - John Heywood

M ost of us consider networking to be a four-letter word. The word conjures up visions of dark rooms filled with overdressed people handing out business cards, and trying to sell you on their newest, latest, greatest product or opportunity. While the prospect of attending one of these on purpose can seem a bit intimidating, I'm going to show you how you can not only survive your next event, but actually thrive.

On almost every chart that ranks people phobias, the fear of social gathering hovers near the top of the list. While approximately fifty-one percent of the population are classic introverts, closer to sixty percent of people consider themselves shy. If you consider yourself to be in that number you are not alone. Barbara Walters, Seattle Seahawks Marshawn Lynch, Gloria Estefan and Johnny Depp all self-identify as being extremely shy when interviewed.

Hopefully, you are using the techniques presented in previous chapters to identify, your why, your values, and your personality type. This self-knowledge is going to come in handy because attending networking events is where the proverbial rubber hits the road. While making significant changes to your personality will take some time, in this chapter we'll cover some work arounds that will allow you to move around the room confidently and get the results you seek. While I'm not a fan of the "fake it 'til you make it" philosophy, I do believe that you can fake it while you are becoming it.

Preparation

There are things you can do before you attend events to give you a bit of a head start.

1. Who are the host(s)? Who are the panelists? Find out as much as you can in the days leading up to the event. No need to hire a private investigator. A cursory Internet and social media search should suffice. Google is your friend. What school did she attend? Do you have any friends in common? Children, activities, etc.

2. Read a newspaper or magazine. It doesn't matter which one. Just read something. The key to networking is being interested in others. However, you must also be interesting yourself. If you are just regurgitating what the talking heads on TV are saying, you are, unfortunately, not going to be very

interesting. Bonus tip: If the function you are attending is for a specific group or organization, spend a bit of time becoming familiar with what they do. No need to become an expert; just know enough to be able to ask specific follow up questions.

3. Rev up your positive self-talk. One of the biggest challenges to effective networking is negative self-talk. "No one wants to talk to me," or "I'm introverted, so I'll just stand here in the corner," or "How soon can I leave without anyone noticing?" These types of voices in your head can completely short circuit your networking efforts before they even get started. Try to reframe your internal conversations. "Someone here needs to hear what I have to say," or "I just need one good connection to make this all worthwhile." Remember, this self-talk goes a long way towards making you appear more confident and approachable.

4. Power Pose - Several studies have shown that simply standing in certain positions can actually change your physiological state. According to the book, Presence, by Amy Cuddy, simply standing like a superhero can raise the levels of confidence hormones like testosterone and adrenaline in your bloodstream before you enter a room, giving your confidence levels a natural boost. If you struggle with confidence in social settings, try this. A few minutes before you enter the room get into what she calls the Wonder Woman or Superman stance for two minutes. If you're not familiar with those comic book characters, whenever either of these two heroes was

about to go into battle, they would take a stand in front of their enemy with their feet a bit wider than shoulder width, hands on hips, chest out and chin slightly elevated.

Entering The Room

How you enter the room can be one of the most critical things you do. The way you walk in the door can set the tone for every interaction you have at the event. Let me explain. While people may not specifically be watching as you enter the room , they will sense the change in energy. As humans, we are wired to notice changes in room dynamics subconsciously. There are some subtle things you can do to make sure you are seen as a positive force and someone people should get to know.

1. Arrive early - Getting to the event a bit early may

sound counterintuitive, especially if you didn't want to go in the first place, but being the early bird offers several advantages. First, you can have a conversation with the host before other guests arrive (you did your research, right?). Second, you can take this time to get to know the volunteers and servers. Why is it important to be on first name basis with the people working the event you ask? Social proof. According to Robert Cialdini, the number one factor people use in deciding whether they like you or not, is if other people like you first. If you are seen as well-known and liked, people will assume you are someone they should know and like. So, when you walk up to the bar and say, "Hey Ralph, can I get another tonic?" and Ralph says, "Sure, Ray. On the rocks?", people will subconsciously think you must be known and liked.

2. The 5&30 Second Rule - If you cannot arrive early, you must speak to the first person you see within five seconds of entering the room. It doesn't matter who it is, what they are wearing, what look they have on their face. Just walk up to them with a big smile and say "Hi! My name is_____." When they respond, follow-up with either, "Have you been here long?" or my favorite, "Are you having a good time?" It really doesn't matter what the follow-up question is, just have something ready. The goal here isn't to have a long, deep conversation. As a matter of fact, it's just the opposite. This initial conversation should only last for thirty seconds. After initial pleasantries, politely excuse yourself. "I'm going to mingle a bit," or "Let me find the bar." Then do the

same thing to the next person you see within five seconds. Do this three or four more times to warm up.

3. Act like a host and not a guest - Have you ever hosted an event? If you have, you noticed how your posture was different; you walked around and made sure everyone was comfortable and having a good time. Where is it written that you can't do that at every event? Taking a host posture is so much more effective for good networking than being a guest. This is all you were doing in the last exercise—acting like a host. Again, what this does it make it look like you are known and liked. Think about it. As you are having your quick conversations, it appears as if everyone knows you. No one else in the room knows that you just met those people a mere moments ago. Unlike high school, you can choose to be popular.

Working The Room

1. Compliments are worth their weight in gold - Think about the time you took picking out your outfit, shoes, accessories, hairstyle, etc. (if you didn't, trust me, others did). There is no better lead-in to a conversation than "Nice _____. Is that _____?" That's it. If someone is wearing something, they think it says something about them, and if you noticed it, you must be a wonderful, interesting person. If you are feeling shy or uncertain of what to say, a compliment is always welcome. Caveat: the comment must be genuine. If you

don't like someone's shoes, jacket, etc. don't try to pretend. People can see through insincere compliments.

2. Do butt in - Sometimes we feel nervous about jumping into a conversation that is already underway. However, if people are there to network, you are doing them a favor. The stated goal of a networking event is to talk with as many people as you can. If people stand there talking to the same person for an hour, it's probably a waste of everyone's time. Proper etiquette for approaching a group is to walk up to them from the front so they both can see you, and stand quietly until there is a break in conversation. Sometimes they will continue talking for a while and ignore you. You can take a hint and move on or do as I do sometimes and change the subject. "That's fascinating! So, how do you two know each other?" Boom! I'm in. Of course, don't be purposefully rude, but sometimes you have to be assertive to jump into conversations.

3. Talk to your friends on your own time - The largest part of the word networking is working. When you are at an event, you should be working. One common trap many of us fall into is seeing an old friend or co-worker and spending the next hour or so catching up on old times. When the evening is up, you're fully caught up on Johnny's baseball accomplishments, and Sarah's upcoming nuptials, but you haven't made any new connections. It's okay to say hi and promise to catch up at a later time, but spend no more than ten minutes in any one conversation. The goal of the night is to gather as

many contacts as possible, not to connect on a deep level with anyone (that comes in the next stage).

4. Keep your hands free - I know it's hard to turn down an open bar and free snacks, but remember you are there to work. One of the primary connection points in making connection with others is the handshake. Done properly, it can send all kinds of positive signals to a new contact. But if you have a drink in one hand and plate in the other, it makes it difficult to shake hands. Of course, if you are coming straight from work it's okay to grab a snack and a drink, making sure that you talk with the person in front and behind you in line. Just don't walk around all night with your hands and/or mouth full; it makes you look unapproachable.

5. The handshake - Once a upon a time, that handshake was a way for people approaching each other to show that they weren't holding a weapon. In more modern times, at least in western culture, it is still a way of showing trust, albeit without the fear of being stabbed by the other party. There's actually some science to the custom of handshakes as well. According to studies, when we touch another human being our brains release a chemical called oxytocin, also known as "the love hormone." This chemical is thought by many to increase trust through pair bonding. In short, we tend to trust others more after we have touched them. The handshake remains a simple way to experience this bond without incurring lawsuits. Bonus Tip 1: Use two hands in your handshake. Don't cover the other person's hand, but use your free hand to

lightly touch the other person's elbow or shoulder during the handshake. Bonus Tip 2: If you suffer from sweaty palms, grab a napkin or two from the buffet or bar, and hold it in your right hand. Switch it to your left when it's handshake time. (There are also some medical treatments for sever sweat; ask your doctor).

6. Let me introduce you to my friend - No sweeter words can be heard at a networking event. Someone has been so nice as to do some of the hard work for you. You now have a certified, pre-qualified contact hand delivered to you. Here's the secret to great networking— you become the introducer. If you've followed most of the preceding steps, you should have connected with 5-10 people early in the evening. Now make it your job to introduce people to your friend to when you think the two would be a good fit.

All Events Are Networking Events

On big misconception about networking is that you have to wait until you are at a "networking event" to begin meeting people. The reality is that you should always be friendly and continuously make friends. When you are in line at the grocery store or cafeteria it is perfectly okay to just say hello. If the person is in a bad mood, no need to push it, but I bet you find that many more people will be willing to talk than you thought. Make a game out of it by setting a number of people to meet every day. Think of these as practice sessions that you can use to build your friendly muscles before you are at a networking event.

Exercises

1. Compliment three people per day. It doesn't matter what you compliment them on just make sure it is sincere. Building your compliment muscle will go a long way.
2. The next time you are in line at a store, introduce yourself to the person in front or behind you.

CHAPTER SEVEN

FOLLOW UP LIKE A BOSS

One of the biggest misconceptions about networking is that it is all about gathering business cards. The more cards you have, the more successful you will be. Well, if you're like most of us with the shoebox full of business cards from people who we have never called once, you know that is not true at all. The fact is that a network is not comprised of how many people you meet, and not even in how many people you know, but in how many people you have a good relationship with.

With today's technology, the problem is not in knowing or being known by people. Most of us have hundreds, if not thousands, of contacts in our phones and even more if you count social media. The problem is in the number of people you can ask for a five minute favor. When you think about the number of people that you can ask for a five minute (or greater) favor, it greatly reduces the number of contacts that are actually part of your network. In this section, I'll show you how to create a self-organizing system that you can use to organize your contacts in a way that will support your goals.

Get To Know Their FROG

The acronym FROG stands for Family, Recreation, Occupation, Goals. For me, these four words act as good reminders to make sure I am covering the bases in my conversations with people I want to grow my relationship with. During the course of several conversations you should seek to learn their relationship status, the number and names of their children, what they do for fun, how they like their job and where do they send themselves in a few years.

These types of questions are easy to ask our "friends" but the goal here is to make your contacts into friends. Remember people tend to hire and promote people who they like and people tend to like people who like them. By asking questions and showing that you are interested in a persons FROG, you are showing them that you are interested.

The Connection Builder

There are four steps to building a connection with anyone. Meet, Eat, Speak and Repeat. In earlier chapters you learned who you need in your network and how to go out and meet them. Now I'll show you the next steps needed to build connections.

Meet - You should already have decided the people you need to meet and figured out where to meet them. Once you have made the contact, decide whether this the type of person that you need to have in your network. If so...

Eat - I've found that starting a relationship is so much easier if you meet over a meal or coffee. There is something about the dining experience that makes conversations flow better. If for some reason you cannot meet in person. A virtual chat will do, but I would encourage you to make an effort to sit down somewhere. Relationships are all about deciding if you can trust a person and there are a lot of non-verbal cues that don't translate well over the phone.

Speak - In order to build a relationship you have to speak often. Many times relationships fizzle because you don't stay in touch until you need something. Everyone hates to get that call from someone they haven't heard from in five years who needs a job. I make it a goal to speak to 150 people a month. Now when I say speak I don't necessarily mean actually talking on the phone. You can drop a short email, text message or direct message just to say hi. Just remember to ask about some part of their FROG.

Repeat - Consistency is the name of the connection game. It is important that you set a goal of contacting three to five people in some fashion every day. To make it easier you might consider using a CRM system to keep track of conversations, or you can just schedule them in your calendar. The key point here is to use some kind of system to make sure you do this consistently. If you touch base with five people per day you will have reached 150 people every month.

Exercises

1. Touch base with five people right now. Send a quick note or text asking how they are doing.

2. Create a contact calendar for the next month. Identify the 150 people that you would like to have an excellent relationship with and put them on your schedule for the month. Now use this as a guide to staying in touch with all 150 of these folks for several months.

CONCLUSION + NEXT STEPS

In the last few sections, you discovered how the Connect Like A Boss Framework helps you build better relationships that will help you move forward in your career. You also drilled down into each of the five core areas—Who you are, who you need, your personal brand, working the room and following up. —and how they feed into the Connect Like A Boss Framework.

You're armed with some powerful ideas of what you could potentially do within each of those core areas so that can leverage your relationships to create the career of your dreams You're also in a better position to analyze where you currently stand and what you need to work on. Be patient Rome wasn't built in a day. The advice I've handed out in this book really help you if you let it.

THANK YOU FOR READING

I sincerely hope you enjoyed reading this book.

I really appreciate your feedback, and I love hearing what you have to say. Could you leave me a review on Amazon letting me know what you thought of the book?

Thank you so much! If you want to get in touch with me directly or get more information from my blog, visit my website rayabram.com. I'll leave a light on for you.

Made in the USA
Columbia, SC
12 August 2020